FANTASTIC FORCES

Gravity

Chris Oxlade

Heinemann
LIBRARY

www.heinemann.co.uk/library
Visit our website to find out more information about Heinemann Library books.

To order:
 Phone 44 (0) 1865 888066
 Send a fax to 44 (0) 1865 314091
Visit the Heinemann Bookshop at www.heinemann.co.uk/library to browse our catalogue and order online.

First published in Great Britain by
Heinemann Library, Halley Court, Jordan Hill,
Oxford, OX2 8EJ, part of Harcourt Education.

Heinemann Library is a registered trademark
of Harcourt Education Ltd.

Editorial: Nancy Dickmann and Catherine Veitch
Design: Richard Parker and Tinstar Design
    (www.tinstar.co.uk)
Picture Research: Erica Newbery and Susi Paz
Production: Camilla Crask
Index: Indexing Specialists (UK) Ltd

Originated by Modern Age
Printed and bound in China by WKT
Company Limited

13-digit ISBN: 978 0 431 18042 7
11 10 09 08 07
10 9 8 7 6 5 4 3 2 1

British Library Cataloguing in Publication Data
 Oxlade, Chris
  Gravity. - (Fantastic forces)
  531.1'4
A full catalogue record for this book is available
from the British Library.

Acknowledgements
The publishers would like to thank the following
for permission to reproduce photographs:
Alamy pp. **6** (Buzz Pictures), **8** (Sarah Hadley), **12**
(plainpicture GmbH & Co. KG), **13** (David Wall),
15 (Darrin Jenkins), **22** (Leigh Smith Images);
Corbis pp. **4** (Reuters/Mohammed Ameen), **20**;
Harcourt Education pp. **9**, **11**, **14**, **17**, **19** (Tudor
Photography); NASA pp. **24**, **25**; Photodisc pp.
7, **26**; Science Photo Library pp. **10** (Professor
Harold Edgerton), **23** (NASA), **27** (Erich
Schrempp).

Cover photograph reproduced with permission of
Getty Images/Taxi/Joe McBride.

Every effort has been made to contact copyright
holders of any material reproduced in this book.
Any omissions will be rectified in subsequent
printings if notice is given to the publishers.

Disclaimer
All the Internet addresses (URLs) given in this
book were valid at the time of going to press.
However, due to the dynamic nature of the
Internet, some addresses may have changed, or
sites may have changed or ceased to exist since
publication. While the author and publishers
regret any inconvenience this may cause readers,
no responsibility for any such changes can be
accepted by either the author or the publishers.

It is recommended that adults supervise children
on the Internet.

Contents

Gravity experiments and demonstrations

There are several experiments and demonstrations in this book that will help you to understand how gravity works. Each experiment or demonstration contains a list of the equipment you need and step-by-step instructions. You should ask an adult to help with any sharp objects.

Materials you will use

Most of the experiments and demonstrations in this book can be done with household objects that can be found in your own home. You will also need a pencil and paper to record your results.

Any words appearing in the text in bold, **like this**, are explained in the glossary.

What is gravity?

If you throw a ball, it falls to the ground. If you ride a bike down a hill, you can move without pedalling. If you pull the plug out of a bathtub, water flows down the plughole. We see events like this every day. Have you ever wondered why? The answer is a **force** called **gravity**.

What are forces?

A force is a push or a pull. Forces make objects start moving, speed up, slow down, stop moving, change direction, or change shape. For example, you push a supermarket trolley to start it moving. You pull the trolley to slow it down and stop it. Forces are measured in **newtons** (N). One newton is about the amount of force it would take to lift an apple.

Gravity is the force that makes you fall towards the Earth's surface. Gravity acts on you all the time. If it stopped you would drift off into space!

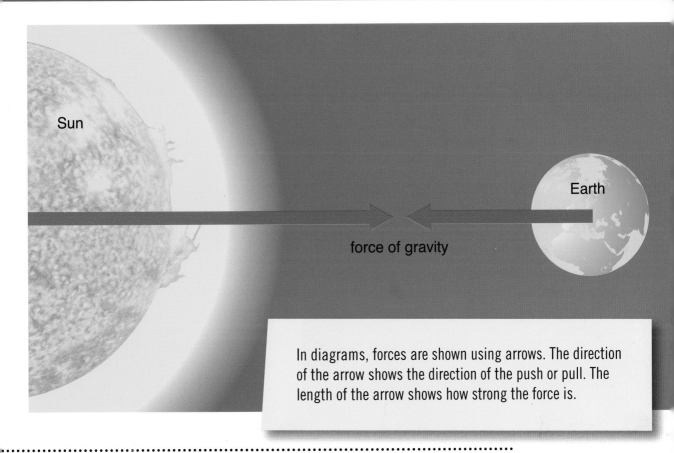

Sun

Earth

force of gravity

In diagrams, forces are shown using arrows. The direction of the arrow shows the direction of the push or pull. The length of the arrow shows how strong the force is.

What makes gravity?

Gravity is a force that pulls every object on Earth downwards, towards the centre of Earth. Gravity always pulls on objects. It never pushes. Gravity actually pulls all objects towards each other. The heavier the objects are, the bigger the pull. The force between everyday objects, such as you and this book, is incredibly tiny. You do not feel it.

Do other planets have gravity?

Gravity is one of the most important forces in the **universe**. It holds our **galaxy** together. The Sun's gravity pulls Earth towards it. It keeps all the planets in our **solar system** going round the Sun.

Why do things fall to Earth?

An object starts to move when a **force** pushes or pulls it. For example, you push a model car to make it move. You then push or pull in the opposite direction to slow down the car and make it stop. **Gravity** is a force that pulls things downwards.

Why does gravity pull down?

The pull of gravity between two objects is always in a straight line. Earth's gravity pulls objects towards the centre of Earth. The centre of Earth is always straight down.

This free-fall parachutist jumped from a plane. Gravity made him fall towards Earth. He fell faster and faster.

What happens when I drop something?

If you hold a tennis ball in your hand, there are two forces acting on the ball. Gravity is pulling it downwards, and you are pushing it upwards. The two forces cancel each other out, so the ball stays still. If you pull away your hand, only gravity is left. It pulls the ball downwards.

An open parachute creates lots of air resistance. This makes the parachutist fall slowly.

DID YOU KNOW?

Forces push and pull an object as it falls through the air. Gravity pulls it down and the air pushes up against it. The force of the air is called **air resistance**. Air resistance slows down the fall of large, light objects, such as balloons. Small, heavy objects, such as marbles, fall much faster.

What happens to a ball when I throw it?

You may have heard the saying, "What goes up must come down." **Gravity** always pulls objects thrown into the air back down to Earth. If you throw a ball straight up in the air, gravity pulls on the ball as soon as it leaves your hand. Eventually the ball stops going upwards and gravity pulls it downwards.

Trampolining would not work without gravity! Every time the trampoline throws you up, gravity pulls you back down again.

DID YOU KNOW?

Gravity stops an object moving up, not along. Throw a heavy ball along as well as upwards. The ball keeps travelling along, until gravity makes it hit the ground. The harder you throw a ball along, the further it gets before gravity pulls it back to the ground.

DEMONSTRATION:

Going up and coming down

This demonstration shows how a thrown object moves through the air.

Equipment: 1 long strip of card, 1 large sheet of card, a pile of books, a marble.

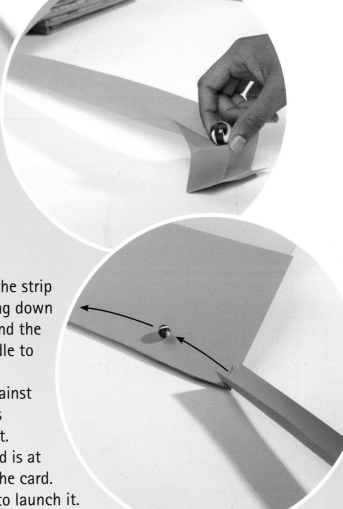

Demonstration steps:

1. Make a launching chute from the strip of card. Make a stand by folding down 3 cm (2 inches) at one end. Bend the rest of the card along the middle to make a "v" shape.
2. Rest the large sheet of card against a pile of books. The card slopes gently down from back to front.
3. Stand the chute so that the end is at one of the bottom corners of the card.
4. Roll a marble down the chute to launch it. Look at the path the marble travels over the sheet of card.
5. Experiment with placing the chute in different positions and rolling the marble faster down the chute. What happens?

Explanation: The marble travels in a long curved path. This shows how gravity pulls the marble down but does not stop it travelling along.

Do heavy objects fall faster?

When a moving object gets faster and faster, we say it is **accelerating**. **Gravity** makes heavy and light objects accelerate downwards at the same rate. Try the experiment opposite. Drop a tennis ball and a heavy stone from the same height, at the same time. They will hit the ground at the same time, even though one is heavier than the other. Why?

The stone is heavier, so the **force** of gravity pulling on the stone is greater than the force of gravity pulling on the ball. You might think this would make the stone fall faster. However, because the stone is heavier, it takes more force to make it accelerate downwards. This means that the stone and ball fall side by side.

This photo is made of many photos taken very quickly. You can see that the ball speeds up as it falls.

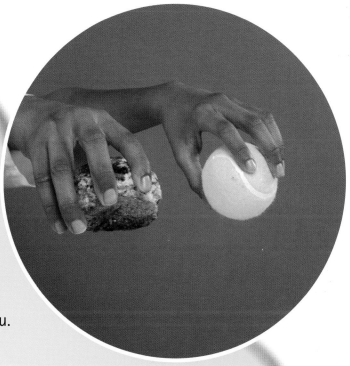

EXPERIMENT:

The stone and tennis ball

Question: Will gravity make two objects of different weights fall to the ground at the same speed?

Hypothesis: The objects will fall at the same speed.

Equipment: Tennis ball, tennis ball-sized stone, a friend to help you.

Experiment steps:
1. Hold the tennis ball and the stone at the same height, one in each hand.
2. Ask your friend to watch the ball and stone carefully.
3. Release the ball and stone together.
4. Your friend should see that they land together.

Conclusion: The two objects hit the ground at the same time, so gravity must make them fall at the same speed.

DID YOU KNOW?

Air resistance pushes up against an object as it falls. This makes larger, lighter objects fall more slowly than smaller, heavier objects. All objects would fall at the same speed in a **vacuum**, where there is no air. In a vacuum, a hammer and a feather dropped together would land together!

Can gravity work for us?

We often use **forces** (pushes and pulls) to make machines work. For example, you push down on the pedals of a bicycle to make it move forwards. Many machines, such as food mixers or remote-controlled cars, have electric **motors** that do the pulling or pushing. Some machines use **gravity** to make them work. The pull of gravity on a weight moves the parts of the machine. For example, a cuckoo clock has heavy weights that gradually fall and turn the cogs inside the clock. This turns the clock hands and strikes the chimes.

This cuckoo clock is powered by the weights hanging underneath!

DID YOU KNOW?

Gravity helps us to make **electricity** for our homes, schools, and offices. At a **hydroelectric power** station, gravity pulls water downhill. The flowing water turns a huge wheel called a **turbine**. The turbine turns a machine called a **generator**. This makes electricity. The electricity can be used for lighting, heating, and for powering all sorts of machines.

The only force making this roller coaster hurtle around its corkscrew track is gravity.

How else do we use gravity?

Lots of things use gravity to make them move. For example, gravity pulls down on the door of a cat flap to make it close. Gravity pulls a roller coaster car down a track, and slows it on the up slopes. You can also see gravity at work in parks and playgrounds. Gravity makes a swing speed up and slow down, as it swings backwards and forwards. It makes a see-saw rock up and down. In lifts there is a heavy weight called a **counterweight**. Some of the force needed to pull up the lift comes from gravity pulling down the counterweight.

DEMONSTRATION:

A gravity-powered model

This demonstration shows how gravity can power a machine.

Equipment: A large metal paper clip, 2 small strips of card, 1 small square of card, scissors, sticky tape, a drinking straw, modelling clay, a small coin, cotton thread.

Demonstration steps:
1. Unbend a paper clip to make it straight. Then bend the last 3 cm (1 inch) at one end.
2. Tape the two small strips of card together to make a windmill sail, then attach the bent end of the paper clip.
3. Cut two v-shaped notches in opposite edges of the small square of card.
4. Push the straight end of the paper clip through the straw and tape the square card to it at the other end, with the notches facing outwards.
5. Cut a 60-cm (24-inch) length of cotton and squeeze a small blob of modelling clay on one end. Cover a coin in modelling clay and squeeze it onto the other end.
6. Hold the straw in one hand and wrap the cotton once around the notches so that the end with the coin is higher. Release the cotton to make the windmill turn.

Explanation: Gravity pulls down on the coin, which pulls the string and turns the windmill sail. The sail is powered by gravity.

What is weight?

The word "**weight**" can be a bit confusing. In everyday life, we often buy food by weight. For example, we might buy a bag of sugar that *weighs* 2 kilograms (4 pounds). In science, the word "weight" means something different. In science, weight is a **force**. The weight of an object is the size of the force of **gravity** pulling it downwards.

Scientists do not use kilograms or pounds to measure weight. Scientists measure weight in **newtons** (N). Scientists use kilograms or pounds to measure **mass**. In science, weight and mass are two different things.

A kitchen scale gives a reading in kilograms (or pounds and ounces). In science, this reading is a measure of mass, even though we call it weight in everyday life.

What is mass?

The mass of an object is the amount of material in it. The mass of an object depends on its size and what it is made of. For example, a small metal object can have more mass than a larger wooden object.

How is weight measured?

Scientists do not measure weight using a weighing **scale**. Instead they use a machine called a **spring scale**. A spring scale gives an answer in newtons.

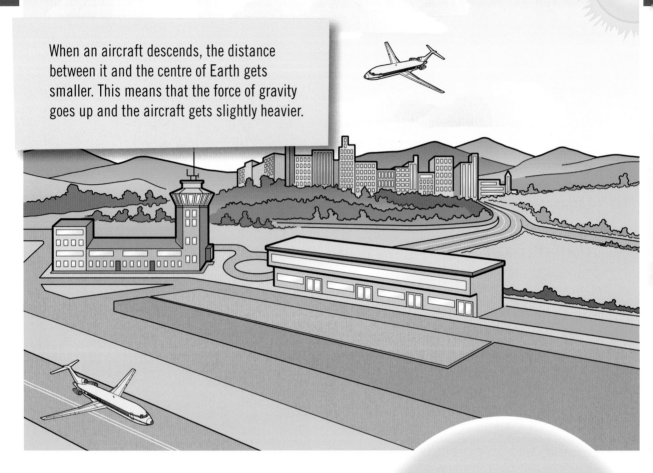

When an aircraft descends, the distance between it and the centre of Earth gets smaller. This means that the force of gravity goes up and the aircraft gets slightly heavier.

Can weight change?

Your weight is the size of the force of Earth's gravity pulling you down. If you go to a place where the force of gravity is different, your weight will be different, too. The force of gravity on the Moon is less than on Earth. On the Moon you would weigh less than you do on Earth. Your mass is always the same, no matter where you are.

DID YOU KNOW?

The pull of Earth's gravity changes. It slowly gets weaker as you move away from Earth. This means that an aircraft weighs a tiny bit less flying at 10,000 metres (33,000 feet) than it does on the ground.

DEMONSTRATION:

A simple weighing machine

This demonstration shows how a simple weighing machine works.

Equipment: A thick piece of card about 20 cm (8 inches) x 10 cm (4 inches), a thin elastic band, a paper clip, some string.

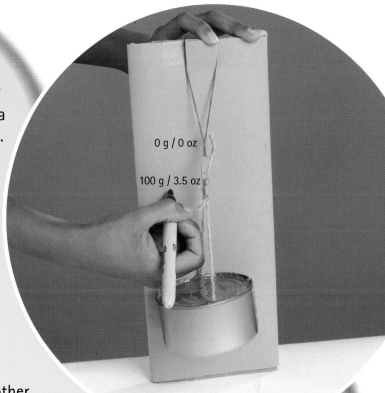

0 g / 0 oz

100 g / 3.5 oz

Demonstration steps:

1. Make two cuts about 3 cm (1 inch) apart at one end of the card. Slot the elastic band into them.
2. Attach the paper clip to the other end of the elastic band.
3. Pull the elastic band tight, but do not stretch it. Draw a line on the card next to the bottom of the paper clip, and mark 0 next to it.
4. Tie some string around a known weight, such as a 100 gram (3.5 ounce) tin of tuna. Leave a loose end of string. Tie this to the paper clip.
5. Hold the card upright. Draw another line and mark 100 grams (3.5 ounces) next to the bottom end of the paper clip.
6. Repeat steps 4 and 5 with other known masses to make a scale.

Explanation: Gravity pulls down larger masses further. This stretches the elastic band more, to reveal a larger mass on the scale.

Is there gravity in space?

Earth's **gravity** slowly gets weaker as you move out into space. But it can still be felt millions of kilometres out into space. The area of space that it can be felt in is called Earth's **gravitational field**. All the **stars** in the **universe** have gravitational fields. So do all the planets and moons. There is gravity all through space.

What orbits Earth?

Earth's gravity pulls the Moon towards the planet. It keeps the Moon in **orbit**. This means the Moon goes around Earth. Gravity also keeps **satellites** and other spacecraft in orbit around Earth. If gravity suddenly stopped, all these things would stop orbiting Earth and drift off into space.

DID YOU KNOW?

Gravity is useful because it keeps satellites in orbit in space around Earth. But gravity makes it very hard to get a spacecraft up into orbit. A space rocket needs to be super-powerful to push against Earth's gravity and blast into space.

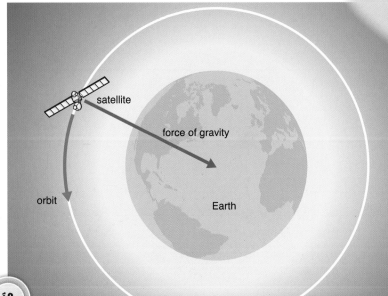

satellite

force of gravity

orbit

Earth

A satellite always moves parallel to Earth's surface. This is because gravity makes its path curve around the planet.

DEMONSTRATION:

Feel the force

This demonstration shows that a **force** is needed to keep an object moving around in a circle. It shows how the Moon orbits Earth.

Equipment: A length of string about 1 metre (3 feet) long, a small roll of tape, a cotton reel.

Demonstration steps:
1. Tie one end of the string to the roll of tape.
2. Feed the other end of the string through the hole in the cotton reel.
3. Hold the cotton reel upright in one hand and the free end of the string in the other.
4. Move the cotton reel in a small circle to make the roll of tape swing around.

Explanation: Imagine the cotton reel is Earth, and the roll of tape is the Moon. You have to pull down on the string to keep the roll of tape moving in a circle. The string pulls on the roll of tape and makes it move in a circle. In the same way, Earth's gravity pulls on the Moon to make it orbit Earth.

In the low gravity of the Moon, astronauts found they could bound about in huge leaps, and carry heavy instruments easily.

Does the Sun have gravity?

The Sun is a star. Its **mass** is hundreds of thousands of times greater than Earth's. The pull of gravity by objects with a large mass is stronger than objects with a small mass. The mass of the Sun is so large, its gravity is enormously strong. The Sun's strong gravity keeps Earth and all the other planets in orbit around the Sun.

How big is the Moon's gravity?

The Moon's mass is much less than Earth's mass. This means the pull of gravity on the Moon is a lot weaker than it is on Earth. The **weight** of an object is the size of the force of gravity pulling it downwards. As gravity is weaker on the Moon than on Earth, objects weigh less on the Moon than they do on Earth. For example, large rocks are easier to pick up on the Moon. You could also jump much higher on the Moon because the pull of gravity is weak.

What force makes tides?

When you are at the beach, you see that the sea slowly rises and falls as the day goes by. This rise and fall is called a **tide**. But why does it happen? The answer is that the Moon's **gravity** pulls on the water in Earth's oceans. It makes the water in them move about.

The Moon's gravity pulls water in the oceans into two bulges. The size of the bulge is greatly exaggerated here.

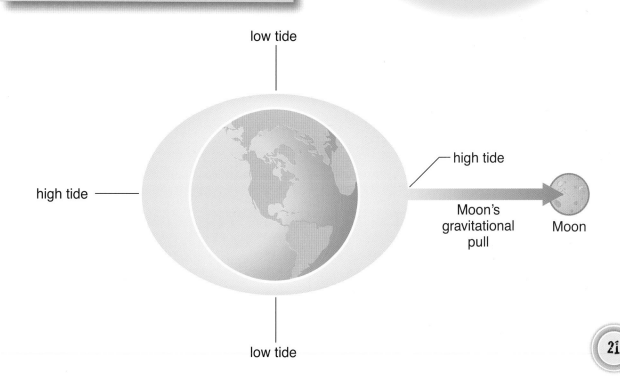

low tide

high tide

high tide

Moon's gravitational pull

Moon

low tide

The Moon's gravity has made the sea level fall here. Elsewhere on Earth the tide will be high.

What effect does the Moon have?

The Moon's gravity pulls on the water on the side of Earth nearest to the Moon. This makes the water bulge out on that side. Gravity also causes a bulge on the opposite side of Earth to the Moon. As the Earth spins once a day, the tide rises and falls twice every day – once when it passes the Moon and again when it reaches the opposite side.

How much do tides rise and fall?

The bulge of water pulled up by the Moon's gravity is only a few metres high. This means that tides only rise and fall a few metres. The Sun's gravity also affects the tides. Sometimes it adds to the Moon's gravity. It makes very high and very low tides called spring tides.

What is zero gravity?

Millions of kilometres away from Earth, far out in space, **gravity** is extremely weak. We say that there is **zero gravity**. If you went there, the **force** of gravity on you would be very small. Your **weight** would be almost nothing! This effect is called **weightlessness**. If you were inside a spacecraft this far out in space, you would drift about inside it.

DID YOU KNOW?

You can feel the opposite effect to weightlessness. When a lift stops going down, the push upwards from the floor gets bigger for a moment. This makes you feel heavier. Stunt pilots and fighter pilots feel much heavier than normal when they make tight turns. If pilots turn too tightly, their blood becomes so heavy it cannot flow up to their brains, and they pass out!

This spider built its web in a spacecraft in zero gravity. It could not tell which way was up or down.

Even though the pull of gravity millions of kilometres out in space is very tiny, it would still pull you back to the nearest planet, Earth, eventually. You would start moving very slowly, but get faster and faster and eventually fall to Earth.

Is there gravity in a space station?

A space station **orbits** Earth a few hundred kilometres above the surface. Gravity is almost as strong here as it is on Earth's surface. But strangely, inside the space station astronauts drift about as though there was no gravity. This is because the astronauts and the space station are orbiting Earth together.

These astronauts are eating a meal inside their space station. Straps on the table hold the food packets in place.

Can I feel weightless on Earth?

You can feel slightly weightless on Earth sometimes. For example, when a lift starts moving downwards you feel slightly lighter for a moment. The same thing happens when a car goes over a hump in the road. You feel lighter because the push up from the lift floor or the car seat is slightly smaller. If the lift **accelerated** downwards as though it was falling, you would be completely weightless inside it!

DID YOU KNOW?

It is not easy to live with zero gravity in space. There is no up or down. Astronauts have to hold on to stay still. Food, drinks, and tools float away unless they are held down. Zero gravity affects astronauts' bodies, too. Some get space sickness, which is like seasickness. They may feel sick, suffer from headaches, or lose control over their arms and legs.

Where is gravity strongest?

In some parts of the **universe**, **gravity** is much stronger than here on Earth. It is strongest of all close to objects in space that have an extremely large **mass**, but which are very small. These objects normally form when **stars** die and collapse.

What happens when stars die?

A star is made of burning gases. The burning gases give the star its power. They are its **fuel**. A star begins to die when it has burnt up all its fuel. When a really big star dies and collapses, the gravity is so strong that all the material is squeezed into a tiny point in space. This is called a **black hole**.

Billions of the stars in the universe will become black holes when they die.

This drawing shows gas and dust swirling into a black hole.

Why is a black hole black?

Black holes are called "black" because we cannot see them. Nothing that is pulled into a black hole ever comes out. The pull of gravity is so high that not even light can escape. We only know black holes exist because we can detect gas and dust from space falling in.

DID YOU KNOW?

If you fell head first into a black hole, you would be ripped to pieces! The strength of gravity changes very quickly near a black hole. As you got near the hole, the gravity at your head would be much greater than the gravity at your feet. Your body would be stretched to millions of times its normal length. This is called "spaghettification", because you would be stretched like spaghetti!

People who found
the answers

Isaac Newton (1642–1727)

Newton was an English scientist and mathematician. One day Newton saw an apple fall from a tree. A **force** must have pulled the apple down to the ground. Newton realized that the force of **gravity** must exist. He also realized that gravity makes Earth move around the Sun, and the Moon move around Earth. Newton wrote three special reports, called the laws of motion. These explain how forces like gravity move objects.

Galileo Galilei (1564–1642)

Galileo was an Italian mathematician. One of his most important discoveries was that all objects fall to Earth at the same speed. Most people thought that heavy objects fell faster. Galileo dropped balls of different **masses** from the Leaning Tower of Pisa in Italy to prove them wrong.

Albert Einstein (1879–1955)

Einstein was a German scientist. Many experts believe that Einstein had the greatest scientific mind of all time. Einstein's ideas include his **theory** that the huge gravity of **stars** and planets changes the shape of space and makes time move faster or slower. Einstein also had a theory that gravity bends light. This was proved in 1919.

Amazing facts

- The gravity on the surface of the Sun is 27 times greater than on the surface of Earth.

- **Comets** travel in giant oval-shaped **orbits** around the Sun. Some travel tens of thousands of millions of kilometres away from the Sun before the Sun's gravity gradually slows them and brings them back.

- Space station showers and toilets have pumps that suck up weightless droplets of water.

- During a rocket lift-off, astronauts feel three times heavier than normal because of the huge **acceleration**. They wear special suits to stop their blood draining downwards.

- One idea about the future of the **universe** is called the "Big Crunch". It suggests that in billions of years' time **gravity** will make the universe collapse.

- Because of **weightlessness**, astronauts get a bit taller in space. This is because gravity does not make their bodies squash their leg and back bones together.

- On a roller coaster, you feel weightless on the humps and heavier than normal in the dips.

- A star that has collapsed is called a neutron star. A neutron star is two or three times heavier than the Sun, but is only a few kilometres across. Gravity is so high that a grain of sand would weigh about a million tonnes.

Glossary

accelerate speed up or slow down

air resistance pushing force of air against a moving object. Force that slows down objects moving through the air.

black hole point in space where all material has been squeezed into a tiny point. Gravity is so strong nothing can escape, not even light.

comet small clump of ice and dust that orbits the Sun

counterweight weight that balances another

electricity type of energy that gives power to our homes

force push or pull that makes an object move, speed up, change direction or slow down

fuel material that burns to give heat or power

galaxy giant group of stars in space

gravitational field area of space where gravity is felt

gravity force that pulls all objects towards each other and towards the centre of Earth

hydroelectric power electric power made from flowing water

mass amount of matter in an object. Mass causes objects to have weight.

motor machine that gives a vehicle power

newton unit to measure force

orbit rotate around a planet or star

satellite unmanned spacecraft that orbits Earth or another planet

scale range of numbers to measure something by. Also, machine used to measure weight.

solar system a star and all the planets that orbit it

spring scale machine that scientists use to measure weight

spring tides very high and very low tides

star giant, glowing ball of gas in space

theory idea that has not been proven

tide when the sea slowly rises and falls

turbine wheel machine turned by flowing water to make power

universe space and all the stars, planets, and other objects it contains

vacuum place where there is nothing, not even air

weight pull of gravity on an object

weightlessness this happens when there is no gravity pulling on an object

zero gravity no gravity

Further information

Books

Fusion: 10 Experiments Your Teacher Never Told You About, Andrew Solway (Raintree, 2006)

Fusion: Roller Coaster!, Paul Mason (Raintree, 2007)

Science Answers: Forces and Motion, Chris Cooper (Heinemann Library, 2004)

Science Files: Forces and Motion, Chris Oxlade (Hodder Wayland, 2005)

Websites

Watch a video of a feather and a hammer being dropped on the Moon at *http://www1.jsc.nasa.gov/er/seh/feather.html*

Find out about gravity at http://library.thinkquest.org/C003108/

Find out all about being weightless on Earth at *http://www.nasa.gov/vision/earth/everydaylife/defy_gravity.html*

Index

Titles in the *Fantastic Forces* series include:

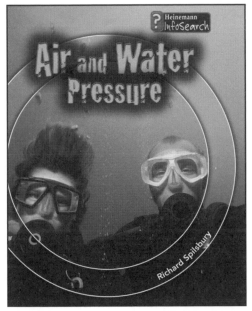

Hardback: 0 431 180407

Hardback: 0 431 180415

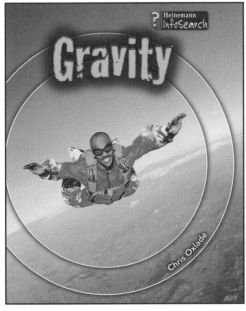

Hardback: 0 431 180423

Hardback: 0 431 180431

Find out about other titles from Heinemann Library on our website www.heinemann.co.uk/library